Everyday History

Telling the Time

Rupert Matthews

FRANKLIN WATTS

NEW YORK • LONDON • SYDNEY

© 2000 Franklin Watts
First published in Great Britain by
Franklin Watts
96 Leonard Street
London
EC2A 4XD

Franklin Watts Australia
14 Mars Road
Lane Cove
NSW 2066
Australia

ISBN: 0 7496 3632 7 (hbk)
      0 7496 3774 9 (pbk)
Dewey Decimal Classification 681. 1
A CIP catalogue record for this book is available
from the British Library

Printed in Malaysia

Planning and production by Discovery Books Limited
Editors: Samantha Armstrong, Gianna Williams
Design: Ian Winton
Art Director: Jonathan Hair
Illustrators: Kevin Maddison, Joanna Williams,
Stefan Chabluk

Photographs:
4 top Clive Hicks/Bruce Coleman Collection,
4 bottom Cheryl Hogue/Ancient Art & Architecture
Collection, 6, 7, 8 & 9 R. Sheridan/Ancient Art &
Architecture Collection, 11 top R. Sheridan/Ancient
Art & Architecture Collection, 11 bottom Mary Evans
Picture Library, 12 John P. Stevens/Ancient Art &
Architecture Collection, 13 top Science Museum/
Science & Society Picture Library, 13 bottom
R. Sheridan/Ancient Art & Architecture Collection,
14 E. T. Archive, 15 R. Sheridan/Ancient Art &
Architecture Collection, 17 top Mary Evans Picture
Library, 17 bottom E. T. Archive, 18 Mary Evans
Picture Library, 19 Science Museum/Science & Society
Picture Library, 20 top Science Museum/Science &
Society Picture Library, 20 bottom Allan Eaton/
Ancient Art & Architecture Collection, 22 Mary
Evans Picture Library, 23 Discovery Picture Library,
24 E. T. Archive, 25 top Science Museum/Science &
Society Picture Library, 25 bottom Mary Evans
Picture Library, 26 Mary Evans Picture Library,
27 bottom Science Museum/Science & Society Picture
Library, 28 Wally McNamee/Corbis

Acknowledgements

Franklin Watts would like to thank the following for
the use of their material: Omega, NASA, Cathay
Pacific Airways.

Contents

Today we measure time in minutes, hours, days, months and years, but people did not always think of time in that way. The very first humans hunted for food or gathered wild roots and berries. They did not need to know the precise time or date. They awoke at dawn and went to sleep when it got dark.

Today farmers still rely on time and the seasons.

Time became important when people began to farm the land. They needed to prepare for the changing seasons, and they needed to know when to begin planting crops, or to begin harvesting. People looked to the skies to help them calculate the time of year.

Stone circles of Stonehenge

There are several stone circles in Europe, but none is as impressive as Stonehenge in southern England. It was finished by about 1600BC. The sunrise on midsummer's day is in line with certain stones.

Nobody is sure why Stonehenge was built. It may have been used as a calendar, helping ancient Britons to decide the correct day for important religious festivals or events.

The solar year

Early civilisations found two different ways to calculate time. The first was to watch the Sun. The Sun rises in a slightly different place during different seasons. By watching where the Sun rose, people would know which day of the year it was.

Spring ploughing.

Late spring, sowing seeds.

Winter gathering.

Autumn harvest.

Early farmers learnt when to plant and when to harvest, depending on the seasons.

Lunar months

The second way was to watch the Moon. The Moon changes shape from full to crescent to new and back to full again over 29 and a half days. The Moon cycle gave rise to months. It is possible that the lunar calendar was in use very early in mankind's history, as early as 30,000BC.

Twelve lunar months only make 354 days while a solar year is 365 days long. Cultures that used a lunar calendar would often have to add extra days to their year to make sure that each of the seasons started at the same time every year.

The ancient world

By 4000BC, people living in Mesopotamia in the Middle East were becoming wealthy. They lived in cities ruled by priests and kings. The priests did not work in the fields, instead they studied the stars and the sky. By observing the rhythms of the stars, Moon and Sun, they were able to work out calendars to measure time.

The Babylonians

By about 1600BC the Babylonians had developed a complex lunar calendar. Each month began with the crescent moon and lasted 29 days. The Babylonians also created a seven-day week. The days of the week were named after the Sun and Moon and the five planets that could be seen with the naked eye.

A Babylonian lunar calendar from the fifth century BC.

Portable time

This pocket sundial was invented by Saxons living in Britain in the 10th century AD. The Saxons divided the daytime into four equal periods known as tides. Each side of the pocket sundial is marked with three columns and each column shows two months of the year. At the top of each column is a hole. When the sundial is held facing the Sun, with a pin stuck at the top of the column showing what month it is, the shadow of the pin shows what tide of the day it is.

6

Since their lunar calendar was shorter than the solar year, an extra month had to be added every three years.

The Babylonians also built sundials which divided the day into sections. The direction of the shadow cast by the Sun told what time of day it was. Babylonians counted in 60s, rather than 10s, so they measured time in divisions of 60. There were 60 seconds in a minute and 60 minutes in each hour and 24 hours in a day.

A Babylonian sundial.

Make a Babylonian sundial

1 Stick a 30 cm piece of dowelling halfway along the edge of a piece of paper or card with modelling clay.

2 Tie one end of a 20 cm-long string to the dowelling and the other end of the string to a pencil. Draw an even semicircle around the dowelling.

3 Position the sundial in a window so that the dowelling casts a shadow in the centre of the semicircle at 12:00 noon. Every hour, mark the position of the shadow on the card.

Telling time by the stars

The Ancient Egyptians were very interested in measuring time accurately and used several different calendars. They used a solar calendar, which had an extra day added every four years to make it more accurate. This fourth year was called a leap year. They also had a second calendar based on the River Nile's annual flooding, a third based on the Moon and a fourth based on the star Sirius.

An Egyptian sky map showing the stars as gods.

Shadow clocks

The Egyptians found new ways to measure time. They invented a more accurate form of sundial, the shadow clock. The shadow clock measured the length of a shadow, rather than its direction.

As the Sun climbs higher into the sky the shadow becomes shorter between dawn and noon, then longer again towards sunset.

Early morning

Star clocks

The Egyptians also wanted to know the time during the night for religious purposes. A star clock was a table that listed the time of night when a certain star rose above the horizon. A person looked to see which star was just rising, then checked the chart to see what the time was. A different chart was needed for each month.

Big dripper

Another way of telling the time at night was with a water clock. This water clock was a bowl filled with water, which dripped out of a hole in the bottom. As the water level sank inside, markers would show how much time had passed.

Noon

24-hour days

The Egyptians divided the day into 24 hours. At first daylight and darkness were divided into 12 hours each. Because the days get longer and shorter at different times of year, this meant the length of the hours varied as well. By about 1200 BC the system was changed so that each hour was the same length.

In classical times

The Ancient Greeks developed many different water clocks called clepsydra. At first clepsydra were simply used to work out intervals of time. But after 300BC, they were used to tell the time of day.

A Greek water clock

One such clock, in Athens, was a large vessel that was filled with water once a day. On top of the water was a float attached to a long rod, connected to a pointer. As the water level fell, the float pulled on the rod and moved the pointer. This clock worked day and night in all weathers.

Make a water clock

1 Fill a two litre (four pint) plastic bottle with water, leaving the top off.

2 Make a small hole in the base with a pin so that the water dribbles out slowly into a washing-up bowl.

3 Using a felt tip pen, mark the position of the water level every minute. Try using the water clock to calculate a period of 15 minutes, then compare this to the real time.

Working against the clock

The Romans used different water clocks for different jobs. Roman senators had a set amount of time to speak. They were timed by a water clock. If they were interrupted, the clock was bunged to stop it until their speech began again. Roman lawyers had water clocks to time how long they spent on each case. For the first time people were using time to control their work.

The Julian calendar

In 45BC the Roman dictator Julius Caesar introduced the Julian Calendar which, with some changes, we still use today.

The calendar began in March, which explains why September (meaning 'seven' in Latin), October ('eight'), November ('nine') and December ('ten') do not correspond with their position in the modern calendar. January and February were the two last months of the year.

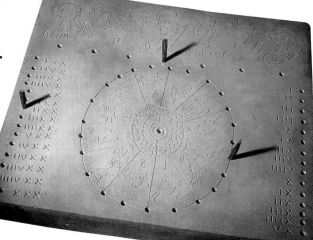

A Julian calendar from Roman times. Pegs were moved around the board to show what day it was.

Pope Gregory

In 1582, Pope Gregory XIII noticed that the Julian calendar was 10 days ahead of the solar time of year. He improved the Julian calendar by removing the leap years from century years, such as 1700, unless they could be divided by 400, as in the year 2000. When the Pope ordered the 10 extra days to be removed, people felt cheated. In England the extra days were not removed until 1751, and even then riots broke out.

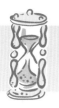

The first mechanical clocks

Water clocks were inaccurate over long periods of time. If they were overfilled, the greater water pressure forced the water through the hole too quickly. Sand-glasses, which had been in use since the third century BC, could only measure small lengths of time. Mechanical clocks were needed that could measure time more precisely.

Water wheels

In AD723 a Buddhist monk in China named L'Hsing tried to solve this problem by using water to drive a waterwheel. The waterwheel was connected to a clock. His attempt failed because the iron wheel rusted.

The Mayan Great Cycle

The Mayans were an ancient civilisation in Central America. They used a sacred 260-day cycle together with a lunar month of 28 days and a solar year of 365 days. It was a complex calendar called the Great Cycle which started in 3114BC and lasted for 1,872,000 days. They believed the world would end at the end of the Great Cycle, on 24 December 2011.

In 1090, Su Song, another Chinese inventor, built a more successful mechanical clock driven by water. Made of non-rusting bronze, the clock ran for nearly 100 years. The mechanism moved wooden puppets to bang drums and ring bells, marking the passing hours. It stood 10 metres tall and included a star clock.

▶ This is a model of the waterwheel that ran Su Song's clock.

Clocks driven by waterwheels were also used in western Europe. Right up to medieval times, Christian monks used waterwheels to power their mechanical clocks.

Water clocks such as this one were used as late as the sixteenth century.

Medieval time

In the thirteenth and fourteenth centuries, the accurate measurement of time became increasingly important.

Church time

Monks, nuns, priests and other church officials were expected to follow a routine of prayers at specific times of day. At first water clocks and sundials were used to decide when it was time for these religious services, but greater accuracy was needed. This led to the development of church clocks.

Before clocks were invented, a monk rang a bell calling his brethren to prayer.

A peasant's week

Peasants working on farms were not interested in accurate clocks. They were, however, interested in the days of the week and date of the year. Some days were festival days when parties and merrymaking took place, and on certain days nearby towns held fairs.

This illuminated calendar from the 1400s shows how a peasant farmer spent the month of July.

Weights and cogs

The first really accurate mechanical clocks were invented in Europe in the fourteenth century. The oldest still existing is in Salisbury Cathedral in England and was made in 1386.

These clocks were driven by a heavy weight attached to toothed wheels called cogs. As the weight fell, it turned the cog and a small mechanism, called an escapement, slowed the cog to a set speed. Without the escapement constantly jamming the cog, the weight would immediately fall down. It is this jamming movement that makes clocks tick and tock!

Early clocks, like the Salisbury Cathedral clock, did not have a face to show the time. Instead, as the cog turned, it drove gear wheels that rang bells every hour.

The age of inventions

In 1583 the Italian scientist Galileo Galilei noticed that a lamp hanging in the cathedral in Pisa took precisely the same amount of time to complete each swing from side to side.

Swinging weights

Galilei began to experiment with swinging weights. His experiments showed that heavy weights swinging freely, called pendulums, could be used to measure time accurately. The time taken for each swing depended on the length of the pendulum and on its weight.

Pendulum-driven clocks

It was not until 1656 that a Dutch scientist called Christiaan Huygens found a way to link a pendulum to a clock. Huygens' invention remained the basis of most clocks for the next 300 years.

▶ The Dutch mathematician, physicist and astronomer, Christiaan Huygens.

Huygens' clock was powered either by a spring or by weights, which turned a cog. This cog was allowed to turn only slowly by an escapement that was controlled by the steady swinging of the pendulum.

A clockmaker's workshop in the seventeenth century.

Exploration and time

From the fifteenth century on, merchant ships sailed regularly between Europe, America and Asia. The ships' navigators noticed that something strange was happening to the time.

Travel trouble

The navigators realised that the Sun was rising and setting at different times depending on where they were. As their ship sailed east the Sun rose and set earlier, but when they sailed west the Sun rose and set later. It soon became usual for ships to set any clocks on board to local time.

Ships in the 1600s had difficulty working out their position without accurate clocks.

Time and position

By about 1700 navigators had realised that they could measure their position very accurately by comparing the time difference between noon where they were and noon at home. British sailors compared local time to the time at Greenwich in England. But nobody had made a clock which would keep accurate time on the deck of a moving ship. A pendulum was useless because of the rocking motion of a ship at sea.

John Harrison

In 1713 the British government offered a large cash prize to anyone who could make a clock that would work on board a ship. In 1773 an English inventor, John Harrison, finally developed a spring-driven clock that kept time so accurately that navigators could find their position at sea even after a voyage lasting several months. Harrison called his clock a chronometer.

John Harrison proudly displays his chronometer.

Time zones

The Sun rises at different times in the world, depending on how much farther east or west we travel. When the Sun is rising in Britain, it is setting in Australia. For this reason, the world is divided into a number of time zones. The time zones are determined by longitude, imaginary lines that run north to south and divide the globe into equal sections. Greenwich was made the starting point of the time zones, thanks to an observatory that stood there in the nineteenth century. Countries east of Greenwich put their clocks forward while countries west of Greenwich put their clocks back.

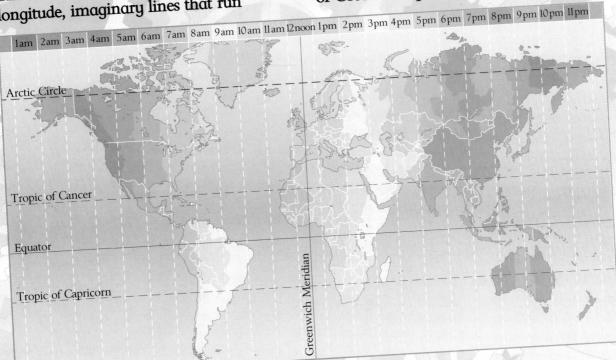

Time in hand

In 1511 Peter Henlein, a clock maker in Bavaria, invented the clock spring and began making 'pocket-clocks' or watches. They were made of iron. Winding up the spring gave the watch its initial movement. They only had an hour hand as the minute hand was so inaccurate it was useless. Even the hour hand had to be put right every day.

This painting from 1558 shows an early pocket watch. It only had an hour hand.

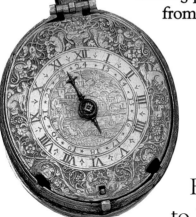

An early seventeenth-century pocket watch from Switzerland.

Watches soon became popular pieces of jewellery. In 1571 England's Queen Elizabeth I had a watch set in a gold case with rubies and emeralds. By about 1660 watches were accurate enough to be made with a minute hand.

Jewels in watches

In 1704 Facio de Duillier, a Swiss watchmaker working in London, discovered that if he set the cogs of a watch on gemstones such as rubies, the jewels produced less friction, allowing the watch to run more smoothly and accurately. However, jewels were expensive to shape by hand so it was not until 1825 that a factory in Switzerland was set up to make jewelled watches.

Status symbols

By 1700, carrying a watch was a mark of social rank. Rich people could afford to have a watch with gold and jewels, which they carried in a pocket. Businessmen had cheaper watches of silver or gold plate. Having a pocket watch showed that a person was busy and important.

▶ By 1904, pocket watches were commonplace among the middle classes.

à la Montre Omega

Wristwatches

People continued to wear pocket watches until the early 1900s. However, during World War I, army officers found that it was more convenient to wear a wristwatch when fighting in the trenches. During the 1920s the fashion for wristwatches spread from the army to all sections of society.

Wristwatches developed during World War I.

21

Industrial time

From the mid-1700s the industrial revolution began to change the way people thought about time.

Factory workers ending their shift, 1910.

Factory work

During the industrial revolution people began to work in large factories. They were paid according to how much time they spent working on machines.

Factory owners wanted people to work in shifts, to keep their machines busy at all times. For the first time in history people were expected to organise their lives strictly according to the time of day.

Public clocks

To help workers organise their time, factory owners and merchants paid for public clocks to be erected. Some of these were placed on church towers, as these could be seen from some distance. Other clocks were put on public buildings.

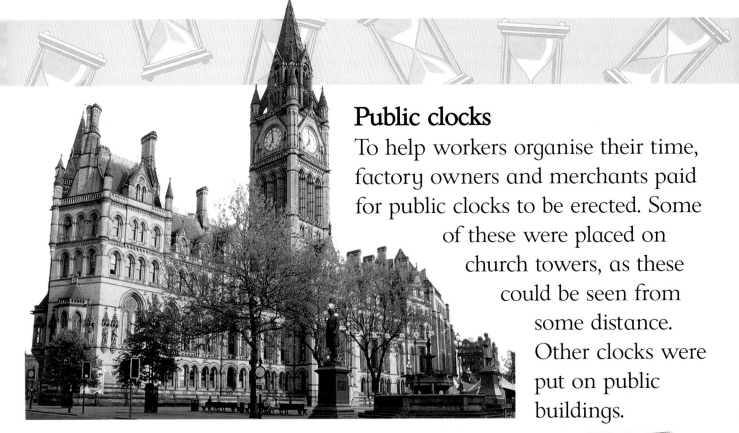

Manchester town hall with its clock tower.

Clocking on

Soon factories had special clocks at the entrance which recorded on a card when individual workers arrived and left. This process was known as 'clocking on' and 'clocking off' and came to dominate the lives of millions of workers.

A worker 'clocks on' by placing his card in a machine that stamps it with the time he arrived at work.

Railway time

The easiest way to find the correct time has always been to watch the Sun to see when it was highest in the sky, which was exactly at noon. In many towns and cities public officials watched the Sun at noon and reset the town clocks accordingly.

However, this meant that even cities quite close to each other had slightly different times. For many years this did not matter. The people in a city used their own local time. But in 1830 things began to change.

Train passengers in the 1830s had to reset their watches on arrival.

Resetting watches

In that year the first railway between two large cities, Manchester and Liverpool, opened to the public. For the first time people could travel between cities quickly and easily. But soon there were serious time problems. Businessmen with watches found that they had to reset their watches to local time for each new city they visited.

Timetables

More importantly the railway companies found it almost impossible to have accurate timetables. A train would leave on a journey lasting two hours, but the different local times might mean that the train arrived two hours and 20 minutes later.

So railway companies began using their own time, which was usually that of the capital city of a country. This meant that trains could run to accurate timetables. But it caused other problems as the railway station clock showing 'railway time' could be up to half an hour different from the town clock showing local time.

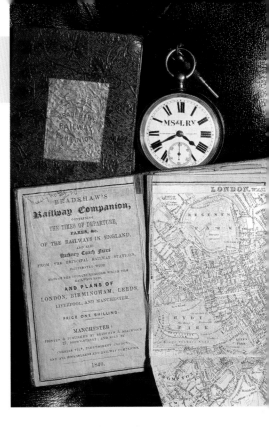

Railway timetables and a pocket watch from the nineteenth century.

London time

In 1880 the British government passed a law banning all local time. Every clock in the country had to be set to railway time, the correct time in London. Soon all other countries followed and each country had its own standard time.

A Paris station clock in 1893 shows railway time.

Radio time

During the 1920s radio stations began to broadcast entertainment and news programmes. One of the first services provided by radio stations was the time signal. People were able to set right their watches and domestic clocks regularly.

In the 1920s people could tell the exact time of day from the radio.

In turn this meant that people knew when to tune in to the radio for their favourite programmes, when to leave for work and when to expect visitors. Everyone had access to a reasonably accurate measure of the same time.

Time for everyone

The development of machines able to produce highly accurate, tiny metal cogs and gears meant that accurate watches could be made cheaply. Nearly everyone could afford to buy a watch that kept time accurately.

By the 1930s, most people living in industrialised societies had become used to living their lives by the clock. They knew at what minute trains ran, when they had to be at work, when films began at the cinema. The idea of judging time by how high the Sun was in the sky was almost unthinkable.

By the 1930s cheap watches were available to everyone.

Quartz time

During the 1940s scientists discovered that quartz had an unusual property. When a low electric current was passed through a piece of quartz, the mineral pulsed at an extremely regular rate. This regular pulse could be used to measure time so accurately that a computer would only lose one second in several years. The quartz clock is now integrated into all sorts of machines, such as video recorders, computers and electronic watches. This is an early quartz clock from the 1940s.

High precision

Modern society is obsessed with time. People need to arrive at work or at school exactly on time, and regulate their meals and breaks by watching the time. Even leisure activities, such as football or concerts, start and finish 'on time'.

The finish line - every second counts.

An athlete's performance is judged to a fraction of a second. The difference of a second can mean a great deal to high-tech businesses which may win or lose large amounts of money.

Atomic clocks

Scientists working on experiments need to time things even more accurately. Some experiments need to be accurate to millionths of a second. To achieve such accuracy, scientists have turned to electronic technology. The most modern atomic clocks are accurate to one second every 1.6 million years.

Losing time

This high degree of accuracy has shown that the modern calendar is slightly inaccurate. In fact the Earth travels around the Sun about 26 seconds a year slower than was thought. This means that in the year 4909 the calender will need to be changed to lose a day. The difference may be crucial in the future, when plotting space missions that may last many years and rely on accurate timing of the Earth's position.

Accurate timing is essential in space.

The more we have been able to divide our time into ever smaller, ever more exact pieces, the busier and faster our lives have become. The more we depend on technology in the future, the more every second will count.

Jet lag

With the invention of passenger jet planes in the 1950s, people often found that they had trouble sleeping after a long trip. Each of us has an 'internal clock' that decides when we should be sleepy or hungry. Because a jet passenger was crossing time zones so quickly, the internal clock could not keep up. The person wanted to sleep when it was time to get up or wake up when it was time to sleep. This is known as jet lag.

Timeline

BC

c 30,000	Humans judge time by the Sun for a daily clock and by the Moon for a monthly cycle.
c 10,000	People begin to use a yearly cycle, based on the Sun, for farming.
c 2800	Babylonians use sundials to tell the time during the day.
c 2200	Egyptians use star clocks to tell the time at night.
c 1600	Stonehenge is completed. The stones are placed so that the time of the year can be found by watching where the Sun rises or sets. The Babylonians use a complex calendar combining a monthly Moon cycle and annual Sun cycle.
c 1400	Egyptians begin using shadow clocks to tell the time during the day.
c 1000	Babylonians develop a method of measuring time using 24 hours in a day with 60 minutes in each hour and 60 seconds in each minute.
c 600	Greeks use clepsydra, water clocks, to measure the passing of time.
c 45	Roman dictator Julius Caesar introduces a new calendar based on the 12 Roman months with a leap year every four years.

AD

723	A Buddhist monk in China produces a water-driven clock.
1090	Chinese scientist Su Song builds the first accurate mechanical clock.
1386	The oldest surviving mechanical clock is built in Salisbury, England.
1511	German clock maker Peter Henlein makes the first pocket watches.
1582	Pope Gregory XIII removes one leap year each century from the calendar to create the modern calendar.
1583	Italian scientist Galileo Galilei discovers that a pendulum takes the same amount of time to complete each swing.
1656	Dutch scientist Christiaan Huygens finds a way to link a pendulum to a clock, producing accurate time-keeping.
1704	Swiss watch maker Facio de Duillier first uses tiny jewels in watches.
1773	English inventor John Harrison produces a clock accurate to a few seconds if kept running for several months.
1880	The British government establishes standard British time, to be set by scientists at Greenwich.
1914	Officers fighting in World War I begin wearing wristwatches instead of pocket watches.
1924	BBC first broadcasts the 'time pips' so people can set their watches accurately.
1951	First electronic computer with built-in timekeeping device on sale.
1991	World's most accurate clock, the Hewlett Packard 5071A is accurate to one second every 16 million years.

Glossary

Babylonians The people who lived in and around Babylon, a great city of ancient Iraq.

Buddhist A follower of the religion founded by Buddha.

Chronometer A highly accurate clock developed in the late 18th century, usually used at sea by navigators.

Clepsydra The Greek name for a type of water clock.

Dictator A person who has supreme power in a country, often a military leader.

Escapement A device for allowing a wheel to turn at a set speed.

Gregory XIII The Pope (leader of the Roman Catholic Church) who introduced a new calendar in 1582.

Jewels Tiny rubies and emeralds used as hubs on wheels inside watches to reduce friction and keep the watch more accurate.

Julius Caesar A general who ruled Ancient Rome between 60BC-44BC.

Lunar Relating to the moon.

Mayans A great civilisation in central America that flourished from about AD300 to 1200.

Mesopotamia The area of the Middle East between the Tigris and Euphrates rivers.

Navigator A person who keeps track of a ship's position.

Nile A river which flows through Egypt.

Pendulum A weight on the end of a rod or chain that is allowed to swing freely.

Pharaoh The king of Ancient Egypt, considered to be a living god.

Quartz A chemical element that vibrates at precise intervals when subjected to an electric current.

Shadow clock A more accurate form of sundial.

Sirius A prominent star that can be used to calculate the day of the year by its position relative to the Sun.

Stonehenge The largest of many circles of standing stones erected by people living in western Europe between 2500BC-1000BC.

Sundial A device that tells the time by casting a shadow onto a marked slab.

Further reading

Hughes, Paul, *The Months of the Year*, Young Library, 1982

Walpole, Brenda, *Millipedes: Time*, A & C Black, 1992

Williams, John, *Starting Technology: Time*, Wayland Publishers Ltd, 1990

Index